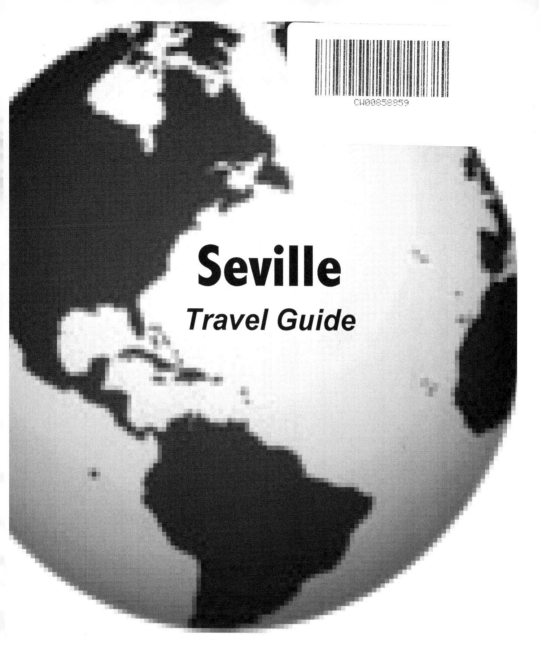

Seville
Travel Guide

Quick Trips Series

Table of Contents

BUDGET TIPS 36

KNOW BEFORE YOU GO 48

Seville

Seville is one of Spain's most impressive cities. The city's Moorish past is evident in its historic architecture and the city had a rich culture even before the Moors invaded 800 years ago. Seville has a world famous cathedral, a colourful harbor and a music-filled nightlife. Its often-perfect weather makes it an ideal destination for those looking to escape the northern winter chills.

Go to Seville to linger in a street café or watch a spectacular bullfight. Experience the famous Spanish tapas (small plates) and a drink a glass of local sherry in one of the restaurants by the harbour.

And don't miss watching the sun set as you take in the charms of the regions famous Flamenco music and dance.

🌐 Geography

Seville is the capital of Andalusia, a province of Spain. The city is located on the shores of River Guadalquivir and is 23 feet (7 meters) above sea level. Seville is the fourth biggest city in Spain with a population of 703,000 in its municipality. There are approximately 1.2 million people in the broader metropolitan area. This makes

SEVILLE TRAVEL GUIDE

Seville the 31st most populated municipal region in the European Union.

The city covers an area of about 140 square kilometers. A large part of the city lies on the eastern side of the Guadalquivir River while the areas of Triana, Los Remedios and La Cartuja are located on the western side of the river. The nearby region of Aljarafe is situated to the western side of the city of Seville.

Together with Genoa and Venice, Seville's Old Town is among the three largest in Europe. It covers 4 kilometers and hosts several world heritage sites including the Cathedral, the Alcazar Palace and the General Archive of the Indies. The harbor in Seville is the only river harbor in the whole of Spain.

🌐 Customs & Culture

Seville is an assortment of modern culture but Andalusian traditions are very much part of the lifestyle of the people in this city. From the famous Flamenco dance, to the street carnivals and nightlife, to the diverse Spanish cuisine, Seville is a city proud of its culture and traditions.

Festivals

The Semana Santa or the Easter Week is one of the most celebrated in Seville. The April Fair or the Feria de Abril is also celebrated during this time, as the blossoming of the orange trees occurs.

Semana Santa started in the 14th century and lasts for 7 days during the Easter season with street processions taking place every day. Many of the streets are crowded by processions of the faithful honoring the Easter season.

Another important festival in Seville is the Feria de Abril,

which began in the 19th century to celebrate the harvest

and the livestock bounty. Gradually, the celebration

became one that honored the countryside of Andalusia.

For the month prior to the actual festivity, the people of

Seville work to create an artificial city of canvas tents

adorned by small lamps. During the celebration, the men

go to the event donned in small jackets, boors and

trousers. The women dress in colorfully as they assemble

to dance and sing.

Cuisine

Sevillian gastronomy is based around domestic cookery and family recipes. The most popular meals are kidneys sautéed in Sherry, Flamenco eggs, fried fish and filled artichokes.

Seville has many high quality restaurants featuring Andalusian, Spanish and many international cuisines.

A preferred method of dining in Seville is to order several small plates shared between a group of friends. This is locally known as *ir de tapeo* (tapas).

When it comes to desserts, the fine savory and homemade sweets made in convents are worth trying. Some of the best are the sweetened egg yolks or the Cortadillos de cidra. Castilleja is a nearby town and is popular for the wide selection of dessert, breads and pastries.

Flamenco

The famous Flamenco dance and music originated in this region. Flamenco is a form of art that is recognisably Spanish since its inception. The Flamenco art form features Cante, which is the song, Baile, which is the dance, and the Guitarra, which is the guitar melody.

Gypsies are said to be the originators of this form of dance and music. Many bars and restaurants in the city host live sessions featuring Flamenco dancers and

musicians.

🌍 Weather & Best Time to Visit

The climate in Seville is characterized by very hot

summers (between June and September). There is little

rain at this time and the temperatures can be as high as

40^0C with a low of 18^0C at night.

The best time to enjoy a holiday in Seville is spring or

autumn when the heat is not as overwhelming.

The winters in Seville are mild and are characterized by

warm but overcast days, phases of sun and clear skies.

Most rain falls from October to March.

Sightseeing Attractions

🌐 María Luisa Park

The Maria Luisa Park is located in the south of Seville, along the Guadalquivir River. It was created in the 19th century and is the main green area in the city. It offers a respite from the sweltering sun of the summer months. The park is decorated with many ceramic benches, pools, waterfalls as well as several monuments.

Some historic buildings can be found in the park and there is a small mountain, the Monte Gurugu. The Plaza de Espana is a large complex in the form of a crescent, which sits at the middle of the main square.

The park takes after the name of the princess Maria Luisa d'Orleans who gave the San Telmo Palace grounds to Seville in 1893.

The three pavilions were designed by Anibal Gonzalez and surround the Plaza de America. This is a stunning square carpeted with flowerbeds and a pool at the center. Each of the pavilions boasts a different architectural design. The pavilions include the Royal Pavilion, the Pavilion of Arts (the archeological museum) and the Mudejar Pavilion (the museum of Andalusian Folk Art).

Address: Avenida de las Delicias

Jardin Americano Botanical Garden

The Jardin Americano is located at the heart of Maria Luisa Park. The botanical garden features a variety of species that were donated by cites of the Americas for the Expo 92. The garden is divided into sections for the various plant species such as cacti, tropical plants and palms.

Some of the plants available here are used for medicinal purposes while others are edible and are used for making Latin American tequila. There are several pools, a lake as well as a waterfall flanked by the bright and colorful yuccas and lilies. Be on the lookout for the tobacco plantations with their large, rough, oval leaves and purplish flowers.

There are benches around the lake offering a spot for relaxation. Close by is the riverside promenade with its wooden bridge situated over the river that meanders through the garden. There is a subtropical section in the garden. A slanting wood roof secludes this area; it also has a pool area and a small waterfall. This area feels like a small version of the Amazon – listen for the chirping of the birds as you look at the ferns, trickling water and lush greenery.

Address: Avenida de las Delicias

🌐 Alcazar Palace

The Alcazar Palace is the main royal place in Seville. It is a large and stunning complex made up of patios and auditoriums all in different architectural designs ranging from Gothic to Andalusian. The centerpiece of the complex is the Palace where King Pedro I stayed in 1364.

When the Moorish royal family took over Seville in 1161, they began to build new structures in the main palace. They built lavish bathrooms, a mosque, towers and a larger palace, the Al Muwarak. Over the years, different royal families continued to build the palace and this resulted in todays varied complex with its mix of architectural styles. The Spanish royal family still uses the upper floor of the palace.

Guests can enter the palace through the Plaza del Triunfo at Puerta del Leon (Lion's Gate). This large entrance is set within a majestic defensive wall adorned with ceramic decorations that illustrate the form of a lion.

The entrance leads to the Lion's Patio and beyond is the Patio de la Monteria courtyard. This courtyard derived its name from the hunters who came to meet the King prior to their hunting expeditions.

The Hall of the Ambassadors (Salon de Embajadores) is the most stunning part of the Alcazar Palace. The building has beautifully adorned archways that lead to a hall that has a magnificent dome built in 1389. The dome displays interlocked wooden panels and underneath are pictures of the kings of Spain.

SEVILLE TRAVEL GUIDE

Be on the lookout for the Galeria del Grutesco a gallery that was initially part of the Moorish palace. From the nearby pond, you have a clear view of the garden. Close to the pond, there are several terraced gardens all of which are linked to each other by gates and small steps. The gardens are surrounded by water fountains, statues and man-made mountains. The impressive Garden of the Dance is adorned with ceramic benches. Within the Royal Garden, you will find several pavilions such as the attractive Pavilion of Carlos V.

Address: Plaza del Triunfo, s/n Santa Cruz

Phone: 954 50 23 24

Website: http://www.patronato-alcazarsevilla.es/

Museum Of Fine Arts

The Museum of Fine Arts is located along Plaza del Museo and is housed in the Convento de la Merced Calzada, a former convent.

The museum is one of the best in Spain and it features a collection of artifacts from the medieval to the contemporary era. The displays here focus on artists including Zurbaran, Murillo and Velazquez.

The revamped convent where the museum is housed was under the ownership of the Order of Merced dedicated to liberating Christian from the Muslims who held them captive. The order became wealthy as a result of the gifts offered by families of those who were liberated. The friars who lived in the monastery were ousted in 1852 and the monastery was transformed into a museum by Juan de Oviedo.

The museum is built over several courtyards such as the Claustro Mayor, the Claustrilla and the Claustro de los Bojes. All these courtyards are accessible to visitors. A baroque porch adorned by intricately decorated column surrounds the main frontage. Inside the façade, Domingo Martinez, painted a stunning dome ceiling, in the 18th century.

The museum has one of the world's most comprehensive collections of Spanish artifacts. These are largely sculptures and paintings from Spanish artists. The works of other local artists such as Luis de Vargas and Juan de Valdes Leal are also featured in the museum. The museum is also home to an attractive display of ceramics and traditional arts made in Andalusia in the 17th to the 18th century.

Address: Plaza del Museo, 9, 41001 Seville, Spain

Phone: 954 78 65 00

Website: http://www.juntadeandalucia.es

🌐 Seville Cathedral

Seville Cathedral is one of the most attractive and largest cathedrals in the world. The cathedral is located in the heart of Seville and was built at the site of a mosque in the 15th century. The Retablo Mayor is an impressive altarpiece lying inside the cathedral.

The cathedral was built when an earthquake destroyed the 12th century mosque in 1401. The mosque that had existed was already considered a cathedral in the later parts of the 11th century after the Christians gained control of the city.

The architect Alonso Martinez designed the grand cathedral and construction began in 1402. By 1517, the cathedral was complete but much of the interior work was not finished until the early 1900s. The interior features five enormous naves. The structure is 126 meters long and 83 meters wide.

The interior also boasts several chapels, an angelic choir and impressive vault ceilings. Some of the chapels worth visiting are the Chapel of St. Anthony and St. Peters. Both these chapels feature remarkable 16th century paintings.

The sparkling altarpieces and the Christopher Columbus tomb are some of the most popular attractions in the cathedral. There are more tombs beneath the altar, where

the royal Castilian queens and kings were buried in the

13th and 14th century.

Additionally, the cathedral houses a museum displaying

priceless paintings and enormous silverware.

Address: Avenida de la Constitución, 41001, Seville

Phone: 954 214 971

Website: http://www.catedraldesevilla.es/

🌐 Italica Archaeological Site

Italica was a vital city during the reign of the Roman

Empire. The Roman army officer, Publius Cornelius, built

the city in 206 B.C. The archeological city is situated north

of Santiponce, 9km from the city of Seville.

SEVILLE TRAVEL GUIDE

Italica was the birthplace of Hadrian and Trajan, the Roman emperors. Hadrian built most of the buildings and places of worship in the city. The pavilion in Italica held 25,000 people and was the Roman Empire's third largest amphitheatre. The amphitheater was the place where numerous performances and port were held and financed by the rich families.

Although the population in Italica was relatively small (not more than 10,000 people), it is clear that the aristocracy was spending excessively and helped lead to its downfall. Santiponce sits over what was once the city of Italica. Italica began to vanish in the 3rd century due to the geological movements of the Guadalquivir River. Additionally, the growth of Seville saw many people moving away from Italica.

Many of the important items from Italica are now displayed in the archeological museum of Seville.

Other important sights in Italica include the mosaic ceramic floors, the statues of the emperors, the public bathing pools and the revamped Santiponce Theater.

Address: Avenida Extremadura, 2, 41970 Santiponce (Sevilla)

Phone: +34 955998028

Website: http://www.juntadeandalucia.es/

🌐 Archeological Museum Of Seville

The Archeological Museum of Seville is one of the best in all of Spain. It is located in the Maria Luisa Park and was initially established as part of the exhibition that took place in 1929. The focus of the displays is Roman history and there are exhibits from the Stone, Bronze and Iron Ages.

The Carambolo Treasure is one of the main attractions of the museum. It is located in the Phoenician civilization section. There are pieces of jewelry on display discovered by workers who were excavating grounds for a new sports field. From the design of the jewelry, Seville's links to the Orient can be seen. This discovery is central to our understanding of the early inhabitants of Andalusia.

The museum's basement displays several artifacts from the Paleolithic era including the Tartessian treasures that were discovered in 1958 in Seville. Upstairs, there are several galleries dedicated to the history of the Romans.

Guests will see statues and various items from the nearby Italica archeological city. Some of these remains include mosaic pieces that date as far back as the 3rd century. Other attractions are statues of the Roman emperors who were born in Seville including Hadrian and Trajan.

Address: Plaza de America, s/n, 41013 Seville

Phone: 00 34 954 786 474

Website: http://www.museosdeandalucia.es

🌐 Basilica De La Macarena Church

The Basilica de La Macarena is located to the north of Seville in the district of La Macarena. It is home to the most respected image in the city, the Virgin of Hope, also known as the La Macarena. It is a holy site to many of the

Catholic faith. The Madonna is seen as the main saint and matador among the gypsy community of Spain.

Joselito, who was also a matador born in Seville, was so impressed by the Madonna that he spent a lot of his wealth to buy four gems for her. Macarenans dressed in weeds for an entire month when Joselito lost his life in the bullring in 1920. Pedro Roldan created the Virgin of Hope sculpture in the 17th century.

Worshippers make a street procession on Sacred Friday each year. The procession carries a statue of Christ and that of the weeping Madonna. The church is not easily reachable by public transport. It is best to go by taxi which will drive through Colon and into Torneo and then to Resolano Andueza.

Address: Puerta de la Macarena

Phone: 34 954 90 18 00

Website: http://www.hermandaddelamacarena.es/

🌐 Torre Del Oro Tower

The Torre Del Oro (Tower of Gold) is situated along a wide boardwalk near the shores of the Guadalquivir River. It is a historic fortress built by the Almohades in the 13th century. The Tower of Gold is one of the most photographed attractions in Seville.

Abu Eola, then governor, built the tower, which is presently a naval gallery, in 1220. The tower was a component of the defense walls that surrounded the city. It was also connected to another nearby tower known as the Torre de la Plata or the Silver Towers; this latter tower is also visible.

SEVILLE TRAVEL GUIDE

In the 11th century, upon its construction, the tower served as a gateway to the port in Seville. There was an enormous chain that linked Torre del Oro with another building across the river. When the naval officers raised the chain, ships would not have access to the city.

Later on, the tower served as a prison and it is claimed that it also served as a home for King Pedro I's mistress. The Tower of Gold has had various uses over the years but today it displays the history of the city's maritime activities.

Legend has it that the tower derived its name from the gilded ceramic tiles that initially adorned the tower. Others claim that the name came from the gold that was excavated from the region.

Address: Paseo de Cristobal Colon

Phone: 95-422-24-19

🌐 Giralda Tower

The Giralda Tower is one of the most popular sights in Seville. It is the bell tower that overhangs the Cathedral of Seville. The tower was initially built in the latter part of the 12th century. Originally, it was a mosque minaret constructed by the Moorish settlers.

In 1356, when the Christians took control of Seville, a large part of the existing mosque was damaged by an earthquake. The only sections of the mosque that were not destroyed were the minaret and the courtyard. The remaining building was cleared out and a cathedral was set up on the site.

In the years that followed, the bronze structures that were placed atop the mosque were replaced by symbols of the Christian faith. The present appearance of the tower dates from as far back as 1568.

Pieces of stones from Roman statues were also used to create the tower. At the base of the Giralda you may still see inscriptions that date back to the time of Augustus the Roman emperor.

The Giralda is so famous that many other towers have been modeled after it. Examples of these towers are the Ferry Building in San Francisco, the Wrigley Towers in Chicago, and Madison Square Garden in New York. Guests can access the tower from the cathedral and through a ramp that leads to the base of the Giralda. This offers a 360 degree view of the city where you can see

other sites including the Alcazar and the Plaza de Toros.

Address: Avenida de la Constitución, 0, 41001, Seville

Phone: 954 214 971

Website: http://www.catedraldesevilla.es/

Museo Del Baile Flamenco (Museum of Flamenco Dance)

Nestled in the interiors of the Alfalfa streets in Seville,

visitors will find the attractive Palace House or the Casa

de Palacio. This building hosts the Museo del Baile

Flamenco (Museum of Flamenco Dance). The building is

dedicated to the art of Flamenco dancing allowing visitors

to witness firsthand the wonders of this unique form of art.

SEVILLE TRAVEL GUIDE

For many who visit Seville, flamenco is one of the main attractions. People love to visit the numerous flamenco bars, known as *tablaos,* to watch local flamenco shows. After you have seen a flamenco show or two and witnessed the gracious dance and music, you can find out all about its history at the Museum of Flamenco Dance.

The museum was established in 2006. Cristina Hoyos is one of the contributors to the creation of the museum. She was born and raised in the neighborhood where the museum is located and is one of the most well known flamenco dancers in all of Spain. Several sections of the museum are dedicated to the legends that she has worked with in building her dancing career.

In this 18th century building, the old traditions of flamenco come together with advanced technology exhibits as well as in contemporary art forms. The museum is popular with young and old who can witness the gracefulness portrayed by the flamenco dancers. The journey into the art of flamenco starts on the first floor where there is an old dressing room, costumes and mementos from the classical ages of flamenco.

There is a movie theater where visitors can view and learn about the history of flamenco. The journey begins from the time of the gypsies who danced just for fun to the present extravaganzas held in theaters and clubs across Spain and the world.

Visitors can see a *tablao* section that resembles a flamenco club. Here visitors can see many famous flamenco dancers who entertain visitors in many clubs across Andalusia.

Afterwards, you may head down to the museum where you can buy music, shows recorded on DVD, Spanish guitars, dancing shoes books, posters and everything flamenco.

Address: Museo del Baile Flamenco C/ Manuel Rojas Marcos 3 41 004

Phone: 34 954 34 03 11

Open: 9am to 6pm November through to March and until 7pm in April through to October

Website: http://www.flamencomuseum.com

Plaza de Toros de la Maestranza Bullring & Museum

The Plaza de Toros bullring museum is one the oldest and most celebrated in the world. The bullring museum is located in Paseo de Colón, and overlooks the Guadalquivir River. It is a great place to enjoy the corrida or the bullfight. Bullfights remain very popular in Seville, although they are not to everyone's taste.

The building features a remarkable façade created in a baroque design. It dates from 1762 and hosts 14,000 people. It is designed to allow the spectators to hear everything. The main entry is at the Prince's Gate decorated with wrought iron.

SEVILLE TRAVEL GUIDE

After an impressive performance, the winning torero or bullfighter is carried through the gate, hauled on the spectators' shoulders.

There is a small museum attached to the bullring. It offers interesting information about the history of the sport from the 18th century to date. The museum also displays memorabilia such as bulls' heads, paintings of famous toreros and their posters, as well as costumes.

Guests can also visit the chapel, which houses the Virgen de la Caridad where the bullfighters say their prayers before the fight. The bullfight season is from Easter Sunday until October.

Address: Paseo de Cristóbal Colón, 12 41001

Phone: 954 22 45 77

Website: http://www.realmaestranza.com/

🌐 Alamillo Bridge

The Alamillo Bridge is one of the most beautiful bridges and is located over the Guadalquivir River, north of the historic centre in Seville. The bridge was constructed between 1987 and 1992 in preparation for the exposition that took place in 1992. The bridge was designed by Santiago Calatrava.

After the river flooded and caused devastating effects across Seville, the city authorities decided to deviate the river westward. The rerouted branch of the river is now known as the Meandro de San Jeronimo. This diversion created the artificial island of Cartuja that derives its name from the monastery in Cartuja.

SEVILLE TRAVEL GUIDE

In 1986, King Juan Carlos I declared that the World

Universal Exposition would be hosted in Seville in 1992.

This event was to celebrate the discovery of the

Americas. The creation of the Alamillo Bridge was part of

the plans to revamp the city's infrastructure.

The Alamillo Bridge is created using cables with its most

outstanding feature being the 466 ft (142 meter) pylon.

This pylon delicately slants at an acute angle and is filled

with concrete to balance the bridge's deck. As such, the

tail end of the pylon does not require any support, giving

the bridge a graceful look.

The bridge looks very attractive at night when it is

illuminated by the lights fitted on the bridge. One of the

best places to have a view of the bridge is from the

shores of Maendro de San Jeronimo.

Budget Tips

 Accommodation

Callejon del Agua Hotel, Calle Corral del Rey

Hostal Callejon del Agua is located in a stylish guesthouse in the heart of Seville. Although the patios here are small, the rooms are pleasantly quiet and offer a respite from the busy streets outside. The rooms are fitted with standard amenities such as air conditioning, a mini bar, cable television and a private telephone.

The rooms overlook the Calle Corral del Rey. The hotel offers complimentary hotel beverages at the lobby, all throughout the day. There is free internet connection throughout the hotel. While they do not offer breakfast, the hotel is near to many local cafes and restaurants.

Address: Calle Corral del Rey, 23 41004 Seville, Spain

Phone: 954 21 91 89

Price: Starting $62 double room

Website: http://www.callejondelagua.com/

Espacio Azahar Hotel, Jesus Del Gran Poder

The Espacio Azhar hotel is located in the Jesus Del Gran Poder area of Seville. It is housed in a historical building giving it a different look and feel from the other commercial buildings in the area. The hotel offers 14 private guest rooms all of which are fitted with plasma television and feature high speed Wi-Fi internet access.

The hotel serves breakfast and guests can have lunch and dinner in the close by tapas bars and restaurants.

Address: Jesus del Gran Poder 28, 41002

Phone: 000 34 954 38 49 59

Price: starting $43 per person

Website: http://espacioazahar.es

Oasis Backpackers Hostel, Plaza de Encarnacion

The Oasis Backpacker Hostel is located off Plaza de Encarnacion. It provides simple but clean rooms at a reasonable price. The hostel is near to a new architectural area of Seville, the Metropol Parasol. There are standard double rooms as well as dormitory rooms for four, six or eight people.

The double rooms are furnished with reading lamps and private closets.

The dorms are fitted with bunk beds with some of these rooms offering a fantastic view of the Plaza de Encarnacion.

Address: Plaza Encarnación 29 1-2, Seville, Spain

Phone: 34 954 293 777

Price: From $21

Website: http://hostelsoasis.com/seville-hostels/

Monte Triana Hotel, Cartuja

The Monte Triana Hotel gives visitors a great way to enjoy the attractions of the Triana district. The hotel has 116 rooms; some are doubles while others host three beds. Guests can enjoy free internet connection and parking. The hotel is close to the World Trade Center, the Technology Park and the Isla Magica theme park.

Address: Calle de Clara de Jesús Montero, 24 41010

Seville, Spain

Phone: 954 34 31 11

Price: starting $29 per person

Website: http://www.hotelesmonte.com

Bellavista Hotel, La Palmera

Bellevista Hotel is located in the district of La Palmera on Avenida de Bellavista which is one of several roads into the city. This chic but reasonably priced hotel is a gem for anyone looking to get away from the hubbub in the city.

The hotel offers 104 rooms equipped with Wi-Fi connection. The hotel serves breakfast, lunch and dinner at the on-site restaurant. There is a swimming pool, a cyber café, as well as a business center and meeting room. Guests can also pay for laundry services.

Address: Av de Bellavista, 153 41014 Seville, Spain

Phone: 954 69 35 00

Price: starting $42 per person

Website: http://www.hotelbellavistasevilla.com

 Places to Eat

Las Coloniales Tapas Bar, Santa Cruz

Las Coloniales (formerly Taberna Coloniales) is one of the most popular tapas bars located in the district of Santa Cruz. When guests arrive at the bar, they write their names on a blackboard and when a table is available, the guest is called to the free table. The restaurant is located in a leafy area and offers shade from the summer sun for guests enjoying their meal.

The food is basically presented but it is prepared authentically and features many Spanish tapas dishes. The sizes of the tapas are impressive and so is the price. The quail eggs served over bread and chorizo is one of the favorites.

Address: Plaza Cristo De Burgos 19, 41003 Seville, Spain

Phone: 954 501 137

Website: http://www.tabernacoloniales.es/

Cafetería Serranito, Antonia Diaz (Bullring)

The Cafeteria Serranito offers some of the largest and most inexpensive meals in the city. The restaurant is always bustling and is located next to the city's bullring. Be prepared for the crowds that throng the area during a bullfight. Some of the dishes served are pijotas, cazon en adobo, dogfish seasoned with local spices, and pez espanada, a grilled swordfish. This is a great place to enjoy local Andalucian cuisine and to interact with locals Sevillans.

Address: Antonia Diaz 4

Phone: 954 211 243

Fogón de Leña Restaurant, Santo Domingo

Fogon de Lena is located close to the Old Town. It was transformed from an old building and now features a wellcrafted, traditional and cozy interior. The restaurant has two stories and is decorated with local artifacts.

Do not miss the chuleton de buey or the ox steak. And, be sure to have a taste of the beefsteak garnished with garlic, parsley and olive oil. The desserts here are made fresh each day and include puddings, pastries, sweets and fresh fruit.

Address: Santo Domingo de la Calzada 13

Phone: 954 531 710

Las Columnas Restaurant, Alameda de Hercules

Las Columnas restaurant is situated along the Alameda de Hercules. Guests can choose to dine inside or outside where there are counters that take your order. The restaurant staff serve with a smile and there is a great choice of traditional meals. The pork sautéed in sauce made from whisky is especially nice. The great thing about Las Columnas is the unbeatable price and its large servings.

Address: Plaza Alameda de Hercules, 19, 41002 Seville,

Spain

Phone: 34 954388106

Cervecería Giralda Restaurant, Barrio Santa Cruz

Cerveceria Giralda is located along the charming street of

Calle Mateos Gagos in Barrio Santa Cruz. There are

plenty of restaurants here but this one seems to standout

from the crowd. The Cerveceria Giralda was opened in

1934 on top of ancient ruins. Today it features columns

and ancient architecture from the 10th century, giving it an

evocative feel. The meals are served elaborately and

include shellfish, codfish fillets, squid, ham-stuffed with

vegetables and grilled peppers.

Address: Calle Mateos 5, 41004

Phone: 954 228 250

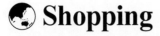 # Shopping

Triana Market

Triana is one of the popular food markets in Seville, located next to the San Jorge castle. The market is a great spot for grocery shopping. The markets offer a wide array of fruits, vegetables, cheeses and hams. If you are looking for a place to buy your groceries for a self-catering vacation, this is a great place to start.

El Jueves Flea Market, Calle Feria

El Jueves is a market located in Calle Feria. The market is open on Thursday morning and offers impressive bargain artifacts such as handmade jewelry, clothing, leatherwork and artwork. There is also a Sunday market dedicated to selling art items such as jewelry, shoes, pictures and sculptures.

Plaza de Espana Shopping, Triana

Artists from Triana have just renovated the Plaza Espana, using ceramic artwork. The plaza, located in the Triana area hosts various ceramic shops including the Ceramica Santa Ana. A walk to the Antillano as well as the Alfareria Street will lead you to various ceramic shops. Every ceramic stall offers something different and this is a great place to buy souvenirs and gifts.

Address: San Jorge 31

Phone: 34 954 333 990

El Azulejo Pottery Shop, Calle Mateos Gagos

The El Azulejo shop is located on the Calle Mateos Gagos, a neighborhood close to the city's cathedral. The shop is well known for its impressive pottery as well as locally made fans. This is a great spot for those looking to indulge in colorful and earthy pottery. The shop is open every day except Sundays.

Address: Calle Mateos Gagos 10

Matador Shop, Constitucion Avenue

Matador, located along the Constitucion Avenue, is an affordable place to buy all sorts of budget souvenirs including t-shirts, wrought iron souvenirs and ceramics. Open from Monday to Saturday.

Address: Av. De la Constitucion 30

Phone: 954 226 247

Know Before You Go

🌎 Entry Requirements

By virtue of the Schengen agreement, visitors from other countries in the European Union will not need a visa when visiting Spain. Additionally visitors from Switzerland, Norway, Lichtenstein, Iceland, Canada, the United Kingdom, Australia and the USA are also exempt. Independently travelling minors will need to carry written permission from their parents. If visiting from a country where you require a visa to enter Spain, you will also need to state the purpose of your visit and provide proof that you have financial means to support yourself for the duration of your stay. Unless you are an EU national, your passport should be valid for at least 3 months after the end of your stay.

🌎 Health Insurance

Citizens of other EU countries are covered for emergency health care in Spain. UK residents, as well as visitors from Switzerland are covered by the European Health Insurance Card (EHIC), which can be applied for free of charge. Visitors from non-Schengen countries will need to show proof of private health insurance that is valid for the duration of their stay in Spain, as part of their visa application.

🌍 Travelling with Pets

Spain participates in the Pet Travel Scheme (PETS) which allows UK residents to travel with their pets without requiring quarantine upon re-entry. Certain conditions will need to be met. The animal will have to be microchipped and up to date on rabies vaccinations. Additionally, you will need a PETS re-entry certificate issued by a UK vet, an Export Health Certificate (this is required by the Spanish authorities), an official Certificate of Treatment against dangerous parasites such as tapeworm and ticks and an official Declaration that your pet has not left the qualifying countries within this period. Pets from the USA or Canada may be brought in under the conditions of a non-commercial import. For this, your pet will also need to be microchipped (or marked with an identifying tattoo) and up to date on rabies vaccinations.

🌍 Airports

Adolfo Suárez Madrid–Barajas Airport (MAD) is the largest and busiest airport in Spain. It is located about 9km from the financial district of Madrid, the capital. The busiest route is the so-called "Puente Aéreo" or "air bridge", which connects Madrid with Barcelona. The second busiest airport in Spain is **Barcelona–El Prat Airport** (BCN), located about 14km southwest from the center of Barcelona. There are two terminals. The newer Terminal 1 handles the bulk of its traffic, while the older Terminal 2 is used by budget airlines such as EasyJet.

Palma de Mallorca Airport (PMI) is the third largest airport in Spain and one of its busiest in the summer time. It has the capacity of processing 25 million passengers annually. **Gran Canaria Airport** (LPA) handles around 10 million passengers annually and connects travellers with the Canary Islands. **Pablo Ruiz Picasso Malaga Airport** (AGP) provides access to the Costa del Sol. Other southern airports are **Seville Airport** (SVQ), **Jaen Federico Garcia Lorca Airport** (GRX) near Granada, **Jerez de la Frontera Airport**, which connects travellers to Costa del Luz and Cadiz and **Almeria Airport** (LEI).

🌐 Airlines

Iberia is the flag carrying national airline of Spain. Since a merger in 2010 with British Airways, it is part of the International Airlines Group (IAG). Iberia is in partnership with the regional carrier Air Nostrum and Iberia Express, which focusses on medium and short haul routes. Vueling is a low-cost Spanish airline with connections to over 100 destinations. In partnership with MTV, it also provides a seasonal connection to Ibiza. Volotea is a budget airline based in Barcelona, which mainly flies to European destinations. Air Europe, the third largest airline after Iberia and Vueling connects Europe to resorts in the Canaries and the Balearic Islands and also flies to North and South America. Swiftair flies mainly to destinations in Europe, North Africa and the Middle East.

Barcelona-El Prat Airport serves as a primary hub for Iberia Regional. It is also a hub for Vueling. Additionally it functions as a regional hub for Ryanair. Air Europe's primary hubs are at Palma de Mallorca Airport and Madrid Barajas Airport, but other bases are at Barcelona Airport and Tenerife South Airport. Air Nostrum is served by hubs at Barcelona Airport, Madrid Barajas Airport and Valencia Airport. Gran Canaria Airport is the hub for the regional airline, Binter Canarias.

🌐 Currency

Spain's currency is the Euro. It is issued in notes in denominations of €500, €200, €100, €50, €20, €10 and €5. Coins are issued in denominations of €2, €1, 50c, 20c, 10c, 5c, 2c and 1c.

🌐 Banking & ATMs

You should have no trouble making withdrawals in Spain if your ATM card is compatible with the MasterCard/Cirrus or Visa/Plus networks. If you want to save money, avoid using the dynamic currency conversion (DCC) system, which promises to charge you in your own currency for the Euros you withdraw. The fine print is that your rate will be less favorable. Whenever possible, opt to conduct your transaction in Euros instead. Do remember to advise your bank or credit card company of your travel plans before leaving.

Credit Cards

Visa and MasterCard will be accepted at most outlets that handle credit cards in Spain, but you may find that your American Express card is not as welcome at all establishments. While shops may still be able to accept transactions with older magnetic strip cards, you will need a PIN enabled card for transactions at automatic vendors such as ticket sellers. Do not be offended when asked to show proof of ID when paying by credit card. It is common practice in Spain and Spaniards are required by law to carry identification on them at all times.

Tourist Taxes

In the region of Catalonia, which includes Barcelona, a tourist tax of between €0.45 and €2.50 per night is levied for the first seven days of your stay. The amount depends on the standard of the establishment, but includes youth hostels, campgrounds, holiday apartments and cruise ships with a stay that exceeds 12 hours.

🌐 Reclaiming VAT

If you are not from the European Union, you can claim back VAT (or Value Added Tax) paid on your purchases in Spain. The VAT rate in Spain is 18 percent. VAT refunds are made on purchases of €90.15 and over from a single shop. Look for shops displaying Global Blue Tax Free Shopping signage. You will be required to fill in a form at the shop, which must then be stamped at the Customs office at the airport. Customs officers will want to inspect your purchases to make sure that they are sealed and unused. Once this is done, you will be able to claim your refund from the Refund Office at the airport. Alternately, you can mail the form to Global Blue once you get home for a refund on your credit card.

🌐 Tipping policy

In general, Spain does not really have much of a tipping culture and the Spanish are not huge tippers themselves. When in a restaurant, check your bill to see whether a gratuity is already included. If not, the acceptable amount will depend on the size of the meal, the prestige of the restaurant and the time of day. For a quick coffee, you can simply round the amount off. For lunch in a modest establishment, opt for 5 percent or one euro per person. The recommended tip for dinner would be more generous, usually somewhere between 7 and 10 percent. This will depend on the type of establishment.

In hotels, if there is someone to help you with your luggage, a tip of 1 euro should be sufficient. At railway stations and airports, a tip is not really expected. Rounding off the amount of the fare to the nearest euro would be sufficient for a taxi driver. If you recruited a private driver, you may wish to tip that person at the end of your association with him.

🌍 Mobile Phones

Most EU countries, including Spain uses the GSM mobile service. This means that most UK phones and some US and Canadian phones and mobile devices will work in Spain. While you could check with your service provider about coverage before you leave, using your own service in roaming mode will involve additional costs. The alternative is to purchase a Spanish SIM card to use during your stay in Spain.

Spain has four mobile networks. They are Movistar, Vodafone, Orange and Yoiga. Buying a Spanish SIM card is relatively simple and inexpensive. By law, you will be required to show some form of identification such as a passport. A basic SIM card from Vodafone costs €5. There are two tourist packages available for €15, which offers a combination of 1Gb data, together with local and international call time. Alternately, a data only package can also be bought for €15. From Orange, you can get a SIM card for free, with a minimum top-up purchase of €10. A tourist SIM with a combination of data and voice calls can be bought for €15. Movistar offers a start-up deal of €10. At their sub-branches, Tuenti, you can also get a free SIM, but the catch is that you need to choose a package to get it. The start-up cost at Yoiga is €20.

🌐 Dialling Code

The international dialling code for Spain is +34.

🌐 Emergency Numbers

All Emergencies: 112 (no area code required)

Police (municipal): 092

Police (national): 091

Police (tourist police, Madrid): 91 548 85 37

Police (tourist police, Barcelona): 93 290 33 27

Ambulance: 061 or 112

Fire: 080 or 112

Traffic: 900 123 505

Electricity: 900 248 248

Immigration: 900 150 000

MasterCard: 900 958 973

Visa: 900 99 1124

🌍 Public Holidays

1 January: New Year's Day (Año Nuevo)

6 January: Day of the Epiphany/Three Kings Day (Reyes Mago)

March/April: Good Friday

1 May: Labor Day (Día del Trabajo)

15 August: Assumption of Mary (Asunción de la Virgen)

12 October: National Day of Spain/Columbus Day (Fiesta Nacional de España or Día de la Hispanidad)

1 November: All Saints Day (Fiesta de Todos los Santos)

6 December: Spanish Constitution Day (Día de la Constitución)

8 December: Immaculate Conception (La Immaculada)

25 December: Christmas (Navidad)

Easter Monday is celebrated in the Basque region, Castile-La Mancha, Catalonia, La Rioja, Navarra and Valencia. 26 December is celebrated as Saint Stephen's Day in Catalonia and the Balearic Islands.

🌍 Time Zone

Spain falls in the Central European Time Zone. This can be calculated as Greenwich Mean Time/Co-ordinated Universal Time (GMT/UTC) +2; Eastern Standard Time (North America) -6; Pacific Standard Time (North America) -9.

 Daylight Savings Time

Clocks are set forward one hour on the last Sunday in March and set back one hour on the last Sunday in October for Daylight Savings Time.

School Holidays

Spain's academic year is from mid-September to mid-June. It is divided into three terms with two short breaks of about two weeks around Christmas and Easter.

Trading Hours

Trading hours in Spain usually run from 9.30am to 1.30pm and from 4.30pm to 8pm, from Mondays to Saturdays. Malls and shopping centers often trade from 10am to 9pm without closing. During the peak holiday seasons, shops could stay open until 10pm. Lunch is usually served between 1pm and 3.30pm while dinner is served from 8.30 to 11pm.

Driving Laws

The Spanish drive on the right hand side of the road. You will need a driver's licence which is valid in the EC to be able to hire a car in Spain. The legal driving age is 18, but most rental companies will require you to be at least 21 to be able to rent a car. You will need to carry your insurance documentation and rental contract with you at all times, when driving. The speed limit in Spain is 120km per hour on motorways, 100km per hour on dual carriageways and 90km per hour on single carriageways. Bear in mind that it is illegal to drive in Spain wearing sandals or flip-flops.

You may drive a non-Spanish vehicle in Spain provided that it is considered roadworthy in the country where it is registered. As a UK resident, you will be able to drive a vehicle registered in the UK in Spain for up to six months, provided that your liabilities as a UK motorist, such as MOT, road tax and insurance are up to date for the entire period of your stay. The legal limit in Spain is 0.05, but for new drivers who have had their licence for less than two years, it is 0.03.

🌍 Drinking Laws

In Spain, the minimum drinking age is 18. Drinking in public places is forbidden and can be punished with a spot fine. In areas where binge drinking can be a problem, alcohol trading hours are often limited.

🌐 Smoking Laws

In the beginning of 2006, Spain implemented a policy banning smoking from all public and private work places. This includes schools, libraries, museums, stadiums, hospitals, cinemas, theatres and shopping centers as well as public transport. From 2011, smoking was also banned in restaurants and bars, although designated smoking areas can be created provided they are enclosed and well ventilated. Additionally tobacco products may only be sold from tobacconists and bars and restaurants where smoking is permitted. Smoking near children's parks, schools or health centers carries a €600 fine.

🌐 Electricity

Electricity: 220 volts

Frequency: 50 Hz

Your electrical appliances from the UK and Ireland should be able to function sufficiently in Spain, but since Spain uses 2 pin sockets, you will need a C/F adapter to convert the plug from 3 to 2-pins. The voltage and frequency is compatible with UK appliances. If travelling from the USA, you will need a converter or step-down transformer to convert your appliances to 110 volts. The latest models of many laptops, camcorders, cell phones and digital cameras are dual-voltage with a built in converter.

🌐 Food & Drink

Spanish cuisine is heavily influenced by a Moorish past. Staple dishes include the rice dish, Paella, Jamon Serrano (or Spanish ham), Gazpacho (cold tomato-based vegetable soup), roast suckling pig, chorizo (spicy sausage) and the Spanish omelette. Tapas (hot or cold snacks) are served with drinks in Spanish bars.

The most quintessentially Spanish drink is sangria, but a popular alternative with the locals is tinto de verano, or summer wine, a mix of red wine and lemonade. Vino Tinto or red wine compliments most meal choices. The preferred red grape type is Tempranillo, for which the regions of Roija and Ribera del Duero are famous. A well-known sparkling wine, Cava, is grown in Catalonia. Do try the Rebujito, a Seville style mix of sherry, sparkling water and mint. The most popular local beers are Cruzcampo, Alhambra and Estrello Damm. Coffee is also popular with Spaniards, who prefer Café con leche (espresso with milk).

Websites

http://www.idealspain.com
A detailed resource that includes legal information for anyone planning a longer stay or residency in Spain.
http://spainattractions.es/

SEVILLE TRAVEL GUIDE

http://www.tourspain.org/

http://spainguides.com/

http://www.travelinginspain.com/

http://wikitravel.org/en/Spain

17603400R00042

Printed in Great Britain
by Amazon